I0841244

FREEING THE MONKEY, SAVING THE PRINCESS

Damián Ruiz

Freeing the monkey, saving the princess

An analytical-experiential method
for the treatment of obsessive disorders

First Edition: October 2014
Second Revised Edition: June 2020
Translation: Benoît du Cann
Design of cover: Cristina González
Layout: Dana Catruna

ISBN 13: 9798583363667

Oriocc Editorial
Guitard, 45, 3
08014 Barcelona
Spain

Printed by Amazon

IF YOU REQUIRE ANY MORE INFORMATION
ABOUT UPCOMING PUBLICATIONS OR EVENTS
AT ORIOCC EDITORIAL, SEND US AN EMAIL AT
INFO@IPITIA.COM

To my patients

For sharing their lives

To solve a problem which has been around for a while, you should change the standpoint from which you view it. Only in this way will you be able to think differently; only in this way, perhaps, you will be able to find a solution.

Damián Ruiz

INDEX

Prologue to the second edition 11

Presentation 17

1. What is an obsessive disorder? 19

2. How does it happen? 21

3. The pathological progression: 27

4. Recurring content in obsessive thoughts 37

5. Is the content of obsessive thoughts important? 51

6. What should a person who suffers from an obsessive
   disorder do? 53

7. What should the family of someone suffering from an
   obsessive disorder do? 61

8. A balanced life: the passion to live 65

9. Tradition as the root but not as the future 69

10. Experimenting, transgressing,.... 71

11. Sexual morality 73

12. Routine and Fear: two forms of paralysis 75

13. Inflexible thought vs. open thought: 77

14. Pharmaceuticals, Alternative Medicine and Nutrition 81

15. Meditation, Mindfulness and Breathing: 85

16. The Role of the Therapist: 89

17. Independence: an important factor in overcoming an
    obsessive disorder 91

18. Dionysian activation 97

19. Why can an obsessive disorder be cured? 103

20. A fairytale as a symbol: 105

21. What is my method for curing an obsessive disorder? . . . 113

22. Many patients: many cures: 117

23. The AFOP method for the treatment of obsessive
disorders: 119

24. Freeing the monkey and saving the princess? 121

25. The second part: 123

Epilogue: 125

Acknowledgements: 127

Prologue to the second edition

Some years ago I started to develop a new method for the treatment of obsessive disorders and I wrote what would later become the first edition of this book. It is an informative book written for patients and family members that explains the circumstances that cause someone with a genetic predisposition to develop an obsessive disorder.

Convinced as I am, like many other psychologists, neurologists and psychiatrists – of the plasticity of the brain, that is, the possibility to generate changes in the brain; I believe in the possibility of curing OCD or improving its symptoms significantly in many cases.

There are many ingrained opinions about OCD and its treatment. Yet I want to present this method and make people understand its mechanisms because it has proven itself effective in a considerable number of cases, something we have seen over and over again at our centre IPITIA in Barcelona, Spain.

Five years have passed since the launch of the first edition of the book. I have presented our method to numerous professionals in psychology and psychiatry, including university professors, and several professional psychologist associations. I presented our method, our data and results from a pilot investigation we did at the European Psychology Conference in Moscow, in July 2019.

We've treated hundreds of patients from all over the world, both in person and online. We've had patients visit us from Canada, Mexico, Colombia, the UK, Israel, China, and the Emirates amongst other countries.

However, none of this can be considered a success. We see it as a responsibility. Because since we have launched our new therapeutic approach, we have to be, and we are, focused on continuing to improve our method, which we have named ***analytical-experiential*** -it has its base in a profound analysis of what caused the obsessive disorder and in the activation of blocked instincts and desires-. We know people expect a good result from us and we put all our efforts into achieving this goal.

This book has been sold thousands of times and it's clear that there is a huge desire from many patients and their family members to find a treatment that will be effective in treating their symptoms. Either to overcome them completely or at least to reduce them significantly. We know this and that's why we are achieving -through research and true effort- more and more advances in this subject.

Finally I'd like to dedicate some words to the Analytic-Experiential theory which sustains our AFOP (Drive, Focus and Activation) method. Like I said before, I started to develop this method some years ago and we're improving it continuously with the entire team. It is now and has been for the last five years, the methodology we follow in our centre.

My training as a Jungian Analyst (I am a member of the IAAP, International Association for Analytical Psychology, Zurich,

Switzerland), and my interest in two other psychological frameworks: those of Theodore Millon and especially primatology (we share 98% of our genes with primates), allowed me to develop a view of humanity which balances between a biological-social-psychological and a transcendent model.

This is why the first step in our treatment is to find out what the detonator was in the person's infancy or adolescence that caused the fear or guilt to appear. After this we work on freeing or unblocking the person from this fear. From here we start working on stopping the process over-adaptation they've learned throughout their life and start to follow the path of individuation. This allows the person not to fall back in a "Modus Vivendi", which is commonly adhered to because of feelings of fear and guilt, and allows them to advance by getting to know him or herself better, all this is done through a thorough analysis of the patient's personal history and through real-life practice and experimentation but I will write more about this in the near future

Foreword by Marco De Colle

Damián Ruiz started talking to me about AFOP, the method he had developed, when he interviewed me for a position in IPITIA. IPITIA being his centre in Barcelona which specializes in the treatment of obsessive disorders.

He explained to me that the vast majority of the patients who came through his doors were people who had been affected by obsessive disorders for many years. They had suffered so much that most had almost lost faith in the possibility of getting cured. I felt very interested in working with people with obsessive disorders however, I had many doubts, since during my years and years of training no-one had ever mentioned that obsessive disorders could be cured.

When Damián explained the logic behind the AFOP method, I was shocked. It seemed as if I had to reconsider everything I had learned about obsessive disorders. I started working at IPITIA and saw that the method was not only logical but also clinically efficient. From there on I knew this was the route I wanted to take.

From a therapeutic perspective the method was very clear, but not strict. It doesn't consist of a rigid protocol, since rigidity is actually what we try to loosen up in our patients. AFOP is a completely new paradigm, a different angle from which to consider obsessive disorders. It requires a radical change in both the therapist's and the client's perspective. Both sides need to be highly involved and engaged. This is the only way the patient will manage to transform themselves in such a way that their anxiety underlying the obsessions and compulsions will be reduced.

Being able to observe how obsessive symptoms are reduced when patients recuperate their instincts, passion, creativity, sexuality and the other elements which are explained in this book, has been a privilege and I am really grateful to Damián for this.

"Freeing the Monkey, Saving the Princess" is a book which I ask all my patients to read when they start therapy. Over time I've seen that they will identify with it in many ways. It is also a book that encourages and provides patients with the necessary hope to change the aspects of their lives that maintain their problems.

Therefore I fully trust that you, dear reader, can take away the same sensations through these pages.

Marco De Colle
Psychologist and Psychotherapist
IPITIA, Barcelona

I discovered psychology, many years ago, thanks to my love of detective novels, especially those by Agatha Christie. When I was seventeen years old, I had read nearly all of them. There were times when I had a fever and I couldn't go to school, I was glad because it meant I could devour– sometimes in just one sitting– a new story by the mistress of the detective genre.

Thanks to Agatha Christie I understood that on many occasions things are not what they seem. I understood that the logic behind certain events goes beyond common thinking and that just because many people may believe the same thing it certainly doesn't make it true. I would even go as far as to say that if an opinion is widely shared, it is most likely an easy solution to a not so easy problem or an implicit pact not to solve it.

More than twenty years have passed since I started working as a psychologist and I can say that what stimulates me most about my profession are the challenges, the difficult cases, and above all those psychopathologies which are considered chronic. Not just because they are intellectually testing but also because there is no greater satisfaction for a therapist than freeing someone from suffering.

I published this book because I believe that, in most cases, obsessive disorders can be cured: I have patients who have made full recoveries, others whose suffering has been reduced to very low, insignificant levels and others who have made substantial improvements. Of course there have been some cases which have been resistant; my current challenge consists of perfecting the method so as to cure those as well.

And if it weren't this way, I would not be stating it so self-assuredly, because it wouldn't be honest, and it would mean tricking people who are in pain, in some cases great pain.

This book is dedicated to those people, to their families, to psychologists and psychiatrists who may want to break away from the official orthodox doctrine of treatments for obsessive disorders, and all those who, for some reason or another, are interested in knowing how an obsessive disorder develops, how it takes hold and how to cure it.

How did I reach these conclusions?

As Poirot, the eccentric Belgian detective created by Agatha Christie would say:

- *"Look without prejudice, simplify your viewpoint and maybe you'll be able to "see" the obvious, what is lurking behind appearances."*

1. WHAT IS AN OBSESSIVE DISORDER?

An obsessive disorder, whether compulsive or not, is a **psychological** illness which manifests itself in repeated thoughts around one or various themes. In those cases where the anxiety is highest it can lead to compulsive acts or rituals. These rituals can be behavioural or mental and serve to reduce the fear which is produced by the repeated thoughts.

In simple words, an obsessive or obsessive-compulsive disorder is the pure and harsh manifestation of an extremely high level of anxiety.

Therefore, it logically follows that if we are able to reduce the anxiety – which can't be controlled by   pharmacological, cognitive or behavioural interventions – we will start reducing the obsessions and compulsions. If we deal with the anxiety, the obsessions will in turn disappear.

Rituals like cleaning something which is already clean over and over again, opening and closing a door several times and counting things or acts, are all examples of compulsions which show the seriousness of an obsessive disorder.

2. How does it happen?

a. Phylogenetic conditioning

When I finished my fourth year of psychology, my biology professor, Dr. Dolors Segarra, solemnly told us: "and remember that a human being is nothing more than a primate with a cultural veneer on top." At that time I already had a more transcendental vision of mankind, more spiritual, possibly influenced by my own search for meaning. I thought that her claim was reductionist and that there was a lot more to it than that. Later, I realized that the majority of psychological theories and ideas were full of cognitive and unconscious elements. Yet very few, took the underlying primate – which resides in all of us- into account. This can cause serious problems in a neurotic civilization such as ours when trying to solve a psychological disorder.

Phylogenetics is the study of human development from its point of origin, from the big bang until now. Our DNA has gone through many mutations throughout our history in order to get us to where we are now. The point is that our DNA carries a genetic memory which incorporates this whole historical process and if you consider that human civilization only started ten thousand years ago, you can understand that our DNA still contains many pre-civilization components. That's why our limbic system (also called our reptile brain) and cerebellum still dominate us on a behavioural level, over our cognitive processes produced by our cerebral cortex.

For this reason, the sobering comment uttered by my professor – without being completely correct – does present an essential element of truth: that we are primates (even though we also have the possibility to develop intelligence, awareness and spirituality). This means that if the primate is not even minimally liberated, in its biological condition and comfortable in its bio-social space, he or she won't be able to reach the higher intellectual levels which have developed through history.

In most obsessive-compulsive cases, our logos (reason), the cerebral cortex, has nullified our internal primate. This is as we've seen before essentially blocking the most substantial part of our genetic configuration. For this reason, one of the first things we have to do when a patient starts therapy for an obsessive disorder is what we could call "freeing the monkey" we all have inside.

b. Ontogenetic conditioning

Ontogeny is what happens to an individual from the moment of conception onwards. There is still a lack of serious research into the moment of conception, that is to say about the environmental, social, physical and parental conditions around it. However, we do have a wealth of information about the development during pregnancy. The emotional and physical state of the mother is transmitted to the foetus. Modern medicine now stresses "no smoking, no drinking, no taking certain kinds of medication or drugs" during pregnancy, but the emotional state is just as important. For example: is this a wanted pregnancy? Is the parents' economic situation adequate? Is the relationship between the father and the mother balanced and approved of by their respective families? Is the mother well integrated within her community?

The answers to all these questions will affect the foetus on a biochemical level. For example, were the mother to experience very high levels of stress during pregnancy this could generate a tendency to nervous irritability in the future baby, beyond any genetic predisposition that he or she could inherit. Therefore, the child will be born with a certain kind of conditioning which will go on to have an impact on his or her infancy. The connection between mother and child, and the emotional connection to his or her family, as well as the stability of his or her environment will all be fundamental in establishing suitable conditions for his or her neurological development, for which it is vital that there is enough mental tranquillity.

As the child is growing up and into adulthood, the impact of the outside world progressively reduces. A traumatic episode at the age of three does not have the same psychological impact as at the age of fourteen. This is caused by the fact that at that age we are not yet capable to reason or think about it in the same way a fourteen-year-old could For example: a two year old boy who lives in a country devastated by war, where he constantly witnesses bombings and adults in states of heightened anxiety, is very likely to develop and generate a mental collapse or paralysis which will be hardly noticeable until he reaches adulthood. Fear will have installed itself onto his limbic system on a deeply unconscious level. his will even be the case if, after having passed through these terrible situations, he will appear calm and tranquil during the rest of his infancy as children tend to do in this case. When he becomes an adolescent the installed anxiety will start to manifest itself and depending on the strategies that the boy develops and the protection his surroundings offer him, the anxiety will manifest itself with more or less intensity.

In many cases of obsessive disorders, I have noticed the presence of traumatic events in childhood or adolescence. They include sexual abuse, serious accidents, the sudden loss of a parent, as well as long term stressful circumstances such as bullying, psychological abuse by the parents, a serious lack of affection, emotional isolation, living in a hostile environment in which parents constantly express hatred towards one another, food deprivation, parents who suffer from serious mental disorders, drug dependence or alcoholism. All this will create a collapse of the nervous system which will force the child to hold back and inhibit him or herself in order to survive this constant state of tension.

That is why our development is very important, especially in its early stages, which include pregnancy and the first years of life up to adolescence. I feel confident enough to say that the majority of obsessive disorders are created in the first fifteen years of an individual's life, even though, sometimes the symptoms do not appear until their early teens. Like I said earlier, we could say that the child or teenager "represses the most instinctive part of themselves, so as to not generate greater levels of anxiety or fear, in an effort to mentally control it." Let us consider an example: a three year old girl lives with her parents who are experiencing economic difficulties. The parents are fighting all the time. They shout and sometimes threaten each other with physical violence. Since this situation terrifies the girl, she unconsciously develops a coping mechanism in which she focuses her attention on the games she has at her disposal in order to isolate from what is happening around her. She is learning to control a situation which would overwhelm her if she did not try to. Let us consider the word "control". From a very young age the girl will lose her natural and spontaneous flare in order to maintain some control over her life. This premature learning will mark her adult life, in which she will unconsciously try to control everything around her. Maybe this could seem an oversimplification, but what I want to get across is that during childhood and adolescence, the person with a future obsessive disorder has already substituted "natural impulses" for "intellect". The question for someone suffering, or a future therapist, is how can you recover your natural impulses? This is what we will focus on now and this e should be the base of all therapies designed for the treatment of obsessive problems.

3. THE PATHOLOGICAL PROGRESSION:

a. Genetic predisposition

With great confidence, as many geneticists affirm, we can say that in the majority of physical and psychological pathologies, your genes predispose you but do not condemn you to develop a disorder. A simple example: if someone has a vulnerable liver due to a genetic predisposition, they might not develop an illness if they try to take care of themselves and watch their diet, alcohol consumption and so on.

With regards to the case we are dealing with here it is exactly the same. Probably many of the people affected by obsessive manifestations may have vulnerable DNA and the tendency to activate this illness, but they don't necessarily have to suffer from it. There is the possibility to reduce stressors, and above all, to activate other aspects of the personality so as to **dilute** them.

b. Repressed emotions

Upon getting an obsessive compulsive disorder, a person has passed through different pathological states, some of which have minimal symptoms or none at all. We have to remember that the incubation of what will eventually become a disorder starts, as I have already said, at some point during childhood or at some moment of adolescence.

Let us consider a fictitious but prototypical example. Lewis lives in a house where his parents are continually arguing. Sometimes he hears his father shout "I'm going to kill you" to his mother. His mother often threatens to leave home. Lewis is five years old and he has been living in this situation since he was able to reason. Given that the tension in his environment is permanent, he has learned not to cause problems, in such a way that he tries to never annoy his parents or make them uncomfortable. Sometimes he wants to play with the small electronic keyboard which he has at home, but he knows that this could irritate his parents. He tries to cry as little as possible and at school his behaviour is that of a model student. However, teachers have told his parents that he is very shy, and that he is very inhibited in how he relates to the other students. At moments like these, Lewis is creating a psychobiological collapse, which , will generate an obsessive personality if he's not liberated, and depending on the circumstances in his life, he could develop something more serious such as an obsessive disorder.

Just to make my point clear: it is possible that Lewis' genetic predisposition is inhibiting his behavior, and that other children would probably be crying, shouting and rebelling, which would cause much more instability at home and more reprimands from the parents. But should this be the case it would save him from this future disorder. To sum up, we are saying that if you express or act on these compulsions, instincts and emotions in childhood or in adolescence – this is basically a guarantee that the child won't develop an obsessive disorder in the future.

c. Anxiety, anguish, sadness, hate and anger:

When we talk about repressed emotions we are basically talking about these five elements. It is true that anxiety is not an emotion, but it is symptomatic of when the other four are not flowing. Each time we feel anxiety it means that some basic emotion was or is being constrained. The expression of sadness is sometimes inhibited because of the lack of adequate receptors. A child cries if they know that someone around them will accept it. If their environment is indifferent or if someone tells them off, the child will learn not to show sadness. The same goes for affection. There are some families who are not affectionate for different reasons. Some because of a social status in which they consider that showing affection is a sign of weakness that makes a person vulnerable, and therefore malleable. In others because they simply do not know how to express it or because the environment is hostile.

Anguish, on the other hand, is a mixture of anxiety and sadness which can very often be reduced through crying. There are, however, some environments which, for a host of different reasons, make the expression of this weeping impossible.

Finally we reach anger, rage and hate. These are the emotions which, at some point in the first stage of their lives, most of my patients had experienced and had repressed. There is nothing worse than being humiliated, harassed, contradicted or insulted and not being able, not having the capacity to defend oneself because that will create a very strong blockage which will generate a lot of anxiety, which the child can't manifest.

I remember an occasion in which the following happened:

A five year old child was playing in the park with other children and suddenly he neared his father, crying, and told him "Daddy, they insulted and hit me." The father responded "Well go back and defend yourself because if you don't do it, I will be the one to hit you". Even though this may seem politically incorrect, something which I am used to, it seemed to me that what the father had said to his son was very wise. The implicit message is the following: "I am here to protect you and I will give you the security you need to defend yourself" and above all "you should be allowed to express your primary drive." It would be preferable for the child to come back having got received a good hiding from one of his playmates than for him to inhibit himself. For this reason, from a young age boys and girls need to learn to express and manifest themselves. Evidently this has to be done within limits: we can't have an aggressive child hitting others continually or a child crying for no reason at all. We have to educate them in dealing with these emotions, not in repressing them.

d. Obsessive personality:

When I used to go to the library – a place where I would go to write (now I go out of the city) – I would sometimes come across this rather strange and curious custom of university students. They would use five different types of highlighters: yellow, pink, green, blue and red. If one of them came to sit next to me – I would usually, if I could, avoid sitting down next to one – the continuous noise upon placing or removing the cap was irritating. *This word in pink, this one in green, the next sentence in red.* It was an encrypted code which only they could decipher.

Furthermore, I imagine that each colour represented something different, which could go from being unimportant to being key. Without wishing to worry anyone – because this behaviour is very regular among some young people – we can say that this is an example of obsessive behaviour. This does not mean, however, that it is pathological.

Here are more examples of obsessive behaviour: people who write out neat versions of their notes taken during class, creating files for each subject, or cleaning something which is already clean, organizing your books in alphabetical order, or organizing your wardrobe according to colour, and so on and so forth. We could easily list a thousand and one cases of obsessive behaviour which is not considered pathological. Until very recently, by way of example, it was common in some families of the aristocracy or of bourgeois society to have living rooms which were only used for special occasions. This behaviour spread to other parts of the population. We could find seventy square metre apartments where the living room would only be used exceptionally. This is another example of an obsessive trait possessed by the owners, or at least one of the owners.

People with an obsessive personality also tend to have serious anticipatory anxiety, that is, they are scared of activities that will happen in the near future. This is due to the need to control everything that is happening and will happen around them. It is about planning your life to such a point that nothing unexpected can happen.

e. Obsessive neurosis

Obsessive neurosis, together with hysterical neurosis, were, in some way, the constitutive pathologies of the Western lifestyle up until one or two decades ago. Since then, psychopathy and narcissism have started to dominate. Put simply, the neurotic obsessive is someone who is continually aware and alert of their actions, about what they mean to other people, of the judgement that others may make and of their possible consequences. It is, using current terminology, as if one was continually in a *casting call*. The difference with the current situation, where narcissism dominates, is a tendency to conformity and unrelenting self-evaluation about oneself. To show the extent to which this is prevalent: in a survey carried out on narcissism with twenty-year-olds from the United States, it was shown that when asked which person they most valued most answered "Me."

Unlike this narcissistic component which is more and more spread out (and which makes people very vulnerable to frustration and highly reactive), the neurotic obsessive is in constant conflict with themselves, their acts and their thoughts. They question everything. If at one point in the day this person briefly raised their voice in a disagreement, they can spend the rest of the day feeling guilty or bad because of this. There is a lot of psychological literature about obsessive neuroses explaining them through sexual repression, repression of same-sex attraction, or ambivalence in affective interaction, while using many different theoretical frameworks

In my opinion, the obsessive neurotic is fundamentally someone who has spent most of their life repressing their basic needs, as much on an emotional level as in the expression of their drives and impulses. That is to say that they become an obsessive neurotic having been through the three points we previously discussed in this chapter.

In Jung's theory a complex is understood as an invasion of "external content", which has not been elaborated by the psyche. For example, someone affected by a *paternal complex* has internalized certain aspects of their father's character and elements of his personality, without having elaborated them into the development of their own personality. This occurs in such a way that there is a massive identification, even unconsciously, with the paternal figure, which on some occasions can be in profound contradiction with the person's potential and non-developed identity. Therefore, the person who suffers from this complex can live in a constant conflict, which can cause them to be excessively controlling.

Now imagine a strict father, conservative and authoritarian in his ways, and a son with a genetic base which leads him to have an experimental temperament with all of its consequences. If the psychological aspects of his father have invaded the psyche of the boy, he will have to repress his real temperamental tendency so as not to be in conflict with the complex. What will he do in this case? He will start to think before he acts. He will think so much that his spontaneity will disappear.

One of the vital characteristics of an obsession, no matter how serious, is to substitute spontaneity for control. We will see that most clearly in an obsessive compulsive disorder. I have already mentioned the idea that the West has been configured with these two patterns: the obsessive neurotic and the hysterical neurotic. In broad strokes, hysterical neurosis is the tendency to express psychic conflicts through the body, especially those of a sexual nature, but also, albeit to a lesser extent, affective ones.

f. Obsessive Disorder

An obsessive disorder develops over time when a person has not found the means to liberate themselves from their impulses, to unblock the collapsed nervous system. The sheer amount of accumulated tension and anxiety behind this collapse has led to an inner tension which can make any event, sentence, word or circumstance get stuck in their mind and become a repetitive thought. It is the clearest manifestation of what we could call the prison of the mind, in which our conscious thought is the prison warden, and the obsessive content **the scream** which the unconscious sends in order to be liberated.

What is this unconscious? It consists of the limbic system and the cerebellum. Both are locked in a dungeon, trying continually to liberate themselves from the tyranny of the cerebral cortex. What should we do in this case We need to reinforce and give power to the limbic system and the cerebellum so that they are able to rebel with such forcefulness that they can overcome the tyranny which conscious thought represents. Here we will not teach the patient to live in a dungeon, nor to conform to it. We will unleash the primary forces so that they produce an authentic revolution, but we will talk about this further ahead.

g. Obsessive-Compulsive Disorder

The Obsessive-Compulsive Disorder is the highest pathological gradient with regards to an obsessive problem. It is the disorder which creates the most suffering in a person I have ever encountered. Here, the level of obsession about something is so high, so strong, that to stop it, the individual has developed a whole series of behavioural and mental rituals, which allows them to escape their repetitive thoughts, even if it's only for a brief moment.

In the 1997 film *As Good as It Gets* (James L. Brooks), starring Jack Nicholson, we can clearly see how someone affected by this disorder would act. One of the clearest examples is when the protagonist walks and tries to avoid the lines which separate the paving slabs while at the same time counting them. Other people who suffer from this disorder need to clean their hands many times in a row, need to pick up and put an object down a certain number of times, or to touch parts of their body in a special order. There are an infinity of possibilities which can be ritualized so that the mind can relax, even if just briefly.

To sum up: What is the symptomatology of an obsessive disorder?

For an obsessive disorder:

In this case, the symptomatology consists of the repetition of the same thought, the repetition of the same word, the trivial acts which produce a conflict or the tendency to do a concrete mental act (add numbers, multiply them, look for a specific number, etc.).

For an obsessive-compulsive disorder:

In this case, we can add to the aforementioned symptoms an act or a ritual which momentarily stops the repetitive thought. In both cases there are different levels of severity. From people whose symptoms are brief, to people who cannot stop thinking and are brought to a state of exhaustion. They waste so much energy on their compulsions that they prefer to keep sleeping or resting all day. In such cases, it is pivotal to release their emotions and impulses as soon as possible so that they can confront the terrible controlling dictatorship carried out by their conscious thought which prevented them from living their lives.

4. Recurring content in obsessive thoughts

a. Being a homosexual

One of the most common and typical subjects of obsessive thoughts is homosexuality. Heterosexual men and women, with a heterosexual lifestyle, who have never felt any type of attraction towards the same sex, suddenly ask themselves if they are in fact gay. This has an impact which appears to alter their biochemistry for a few moments and from that point on the doubt remains engraved. After this, this repetitive doubt returns whenever they're confronted with any attractive individual of the same gender, be it in real life, on television, at the cinema, etc.

The nervous system is so deeply affected by this doubt that there are people who even begin to feel a tingling sensation in their genital area. This increases their angst about the possibility of being gay even further.

Before continuing with this, I would like to ask the following question: why has no homosexual person, accepting or not of their own homosexuality, had obsessive thoughts about it? That is to say, I have treated homosexuals with obsessive disorders, but the topic of sexuality or their sexual orientation was never the motive of the recurrent thought. Also, it is important to point out that sexual tendencies are "inevitable", and can be dealt with in many ways, but what you can not do is lie to yourself.

A couple of American psychiatrists, Masters and Johnson, showed that the general population is distributed on a gradient of sexual orientation, which they measured from 1 to 7, from pure heterosexuality to pure homosexuality, passing through different levels of bisexuality. This, which at the time caused a slight scandal in the North American population and had been previously formulated by Kinsey, is in reality quite a fair representation of the population at large, distributing the population into more or less percentage slices from pure homosexuality to pure heterosexuality.

It is widely known that approximately ten percent of the male population and about five per cent of the female population is homosexual. The only thing which varies from society to society is its visibility.

The first question I asked myself upon treating my first obsessive patients with homosexual content was the simplest: "Are they homosexuals who either don't know it or are scared, terrorised by the possibility of discovering such a tendency within themselves?" I would like to point out that the great majority of these patients had satisfying sex lives with people of the opposite sex. There was, however, something which caught my attention: they were moralists. For example, the idea of infidelity to them was something which bothered them greatly. This differentiated them from other sectors of the heterosexual population who were relaxed with the idea of having sex with a third person, outside of their relationships, or in a more flexible and playful way.

What exactly is going on here?

To begin with, we must return to the idea of the prison and the warden. Imagine that we have these primary impulses and drives, including sexual ones, incredibly repressed due to a blockage whose causes, as previously mentioned, are stressful environmental circumstances or a traumatic event experienced during childhood or adolescence.

Among these primary impulses there is sexuality. While sexuality can be repressed, on an unconscious level, there is the need for freedom.

It is the unconscious, a biochemical area of our brain, which will start to send tormenting messages: "Am I gay?" "Did I like that man?" "Would I like to fellate another man?" etc.

Why do these messages appear? Because there is a part of the obsessive person which is revealing itself against such a level of repression, against such prejudice and against such fear to live. But what part is this? Repressed homosexuality? **NO.** Repressed vitality, assertiveness, instincts and liberty. What I mean is that you have stopped living and you only think. You do not live life, you think it, and your unconscious will not stop bothering you until you are radically honest with yourself.

By way of example, imagine a typical teenage boy who really likes girls, but who is very shy, inhibited, formal and obeys his parents. His classmates start to bully him using insults which question his sexual orientation. In a very basic way, and completely unjustifiably, his classmates are pressuring him into adopting a more assertive attitude towards girls, they force him to free himself and show himself more confident with the opposite sex. This young man can do two things: he can block himself off even more and eventually isolate himself, or he can overcome the challenge and be braver and try to connect with girls in a more secure way. Very much the same thing is happening with homosexual obsessive thoughts. It is nothing more than an attack by the unconscious, and I repeat, so that the person who is suffering can free their heterosexuality, their uncomplicated masculinity, and therefore become someone who is more strong-minded, free, daring and freed of prejudice.

Why don't homosexuals have obsessive content about homosexuality but heterosexuals do?

I have never treated, as I previously mentioned, a homosexual who has homosexual obsessions. Neither have I ever treated a heterosexual with homosexual obsessions who turned out to be gay. I know that everyone who has this problem thinks that they might be the exception. NO. There are no exceptions. And so why do homosexuals not have homosexual obsessive fears? There is a very logical answer: because there is no conflict between one's natural impulses and the content of one's thoughts. It would be absurd. Would we become conflicted by liking apples and having one in front of us? No.

To clarify a point, homosexuality, and bisexuality too, are normal sexual tendencies, without any pathological component, and have existed in parts of the population throughout our history and in every culture that history has produced. Those regressive societies who force people to live in secrecy are an altogether different subject . The excess of promiscuity and sexual compulsion which currently exists in our society does seem pathological to me but that is a separate topic.

b. Harming someone

This could be said to be the second most prevalent content in obsessive thoughts. There are people who are afraid that they will physically hurt someone, be it because they lose control, take out a knife and attack someone, or that they hit someone with their car, physically assault them, burn their house down, throw someone under metro lines, etc. In reality, this fear is once again hiding a repressed impulse. In this case we are clearly referring to aggression.

The continued repression of aggression which comes from being in a certain kind of home or school environment can generate anxiety, which in turn creates a blockage that eventually translates into obsessive thoughts. We have already talked about rigid and authoritarian families and bullying. Therefore, if someone is afraid of inflicting physical harm on someone, we are faced with a person who is repressing their aggression.

This repression does not mean that the accumulated aggression is very high. What is probably happening is that there is no way to express it. Take, for example: one teenager, says to another, *"Are you stupid or something?"* The other, instead of answering *"You're the stupid one"* for example, simply represses it and stays quiet. What will happen in this case?? This kind of behaviour, this lack of a response, can transform itself into an internalized hatred due to the feeling of impotence which the teenager feels towards the boy who taunted him. If this were to happen a lot, with different people and over a long period of time, this person could not only internalize his feelings of aggression, but also his assertiveness, that of saying directly what he thinks, or answering back when he feels verbally attacked. It is exactly because of this cumulative repression that there will be a moment when the imagination of the obsessive individual starts to elaborate excessively violent fantasies.

c. Fear of being a paedophile:

Another very common obsessive fantasy, and one of the most torturous for those who suffer from it, is the fear of being excited by children, especially one's own children.

This fear can be paralyzing; it can lead to a person distancing themselves from their children, to the point in some cases of not being able to see their very young children naked. When a mother or a father comes to me and confesses such a thing, they are terrified that I, in this case in my capacity as a therapist, will judge them and consider them sexual perverts.

The fear of being a paedophile is very similar to the fear of being a homosexual. At this point I would like to stress that paedophilia is a disease and that homosexuality is not. The difference between these fears is that in this case the level of anguish is much higher, and reaches unbearable levels for those who suffer from it.

For those who suffer from this fear, the level of repression is incredibly high. In many cases, the unconscious conflict can be very deep-rooted. In a number of my patients with this obsession, though not in all of them, I noticed that they had had an unhappy childhood. They were not given the opportunity to be children because either they were abused physically or psychologically, or had lived in a household where money and/or affection were scarce. As a result their childhood is in a sense pending. There might be an unconscious and deep part of themselves which considers itself incapable of giving something that they had never received: love, patience, and devotion. From this point the obsessive fear appears: "let's see if you desire your children sexually", which from what we now know could be translated to: "you need to be able to receive the love you did not get, the care that was not given to you, the liberty you never had, so that you can love, without feeling conflicted, your children or children in general".

As I have said before: all of my patients who have suffered from this particular obsessive fear – there have been a few over the years, all of them excellent people and with a great desire to escape from it so that they could love their children – have been able to break out from this alien and torturing thought. But only once their own needs were recognized and efforts were made to satisfy them was this possible.

It is also possible that women in some cases, but mainly men, can reach a high level of repression when they are trapped in a "cowardice" life", due to being overprotected in their childhood. As well as living excessively "standard" lives trying to adhere to a certain idea of perfection. They try to be good husbands, good parents, good children and good employees. This repression can cause doubts about something so instinctive as the object of our desire. But these doubts are caused by inhibition. There is nothing perverse in the person. And the moment they are able to free themselves from this way of living they will see that there is no reason to worry about this. They will become capable persons with a healthy social life and physical strength and their terror about possibly being a paedophile will disappear.

d. What will they think of me?

There is a fine line between an obsessive neurosis and an obsessive disorder, which manifests itself in the thought that you have said something inappropriate, or have offended someone, or that you have done something which is annoying to another person.

In general, those affected by this kind of thinking are in the former category, that of an

obsessive neurosis. However there are people who have this to an extreme level and cannot stop continually thinking about what they have said or done. This goes from being an interior conflict to a reiterative thought. In this case we are dealing with insecure and immature personalities who, despite having entered adulthood, still have a childish attitude towards others and society in general.

This childish attitude often comes from an overprotective and moralistic education. This didactic style creates extremely fragile children, to whom the need to compete in the society in which we live – in essence a civilized jungle – has not been taught. They have many difficulties in getting ahead and they usually stay in second place due to the fact that they need a chorus of approval to validate every one of their actions. Unless they meet untrustworthy or undiplomatic personalities they will start to inhibit themselves and to get into conflict with themselves.

Add to this the fact that social conditioning also generates a high level of repression in the most vulnerable citizens of a society. There are two tyrannical ideologies in different geographic areas of the planet:

- In Europe and North America: the tyranny of political correctness. Freedom of expression is being seriously threatened by political forces who seek to impede free opinion about a variety of different subjects. This puts citizens, as well as the media outlets, under incredible pressure to think and express themselves in only a certain way. They are not able to question individual or collective behaviour for fear of being considered incorrect. This tyranny pressures people's psyche, bringing them to an individual and social silence, and thus permitting negligence, "do-goodery" and permissiveness to become the predominant values in these parts of the world.

- In South America: the ubiquity in some countries of the more strict Christian morality can be suffocating. The idea of sin menaces all kinds of free behaviour; and instead of expressing their Christianity in an integrated and calm way it is lived compulsively. The concept of God is used in everything and essentially to regulate behaviours. In the process it anguishes many people who do not feel the freedom which comes from an ethical life free from unnecessary prejudice.

One has to be conscious about all these things and try to internally free oneself from manipulators and tyrants of any kind.

e. "What will they say about me?"

This is one of the biggest conditioners of behaviour which a human being can experience. In the West, especially in the Catholic tradition, people act according to a moral standard supposedly observed by others – that is to say in the collective imagination – in which the rest of the population has a single common view about events. This moral standard is generally very conservative. As we analyse this, we realise that this makes little if any sense, because everyone perceives reality in a different way, and for this reason we all have different lifestyles and behave differently. This means that when confronted with any action a person does, people will have differing perspectives on it. For example, if we are walking down the road, and we see someone who is dressed outlandishly and in bright colours, the judgment this person will incur will vary according to the people this person encounters. Some will think it fine, others grotesque or ridiculous, while others may consider it fun and original. This same thing will happen if someone starts to act in an eccentric manner or if two people of any gender engage in passionate public displays of affection: some will think it vulgar, others will find it romantic. For this very reason it is important to be clear about the fact that people have different visions of reality, different tastes, different feelings, which not everyone will like. No matter what we do, due to simple biochemical affinity, there will be people who will be very critical of us, and others who will like and tolerate everything we do. For this reason freeing yourself from worrying about what they will say about you is one of the basic principles of liberty. This is possibly one of the most widespread obsessive contents, although it is not the one which generates the most anxiety.

f. Guilt

On many occasions when working with people who suffer from an obsessive disorder I have found guilt to be very present, but often without any actual connection to real past events. It is almost as if this guilt ignores reality and that it possesses existential connotations. It is an imminent guilt, which is in some way linked to certain life circumstances, but without a direct connection. For example, the case of someone who lost a loved one when they were a child or teenager. Over the years this has generated a chain reaction of events which has made them think that in some way they are to blame for the death, even though they had nothing to do with it. Sometimes this guilt can be generated by the person experiencing feelings of hate towards the deceased. In everyone suffering from a guilt obsession there tends to be a strict underlying moral code. You can only free yourself from this by acquiring a more complex vision of existence and activating your Eros, the Dionysian aspects of your nature. We will delve deeper into this later.

But it could be the case that someone actually has done something in their past which they regret. Unless it is a serious illegal offence (not stealing a bag of sweets when they were a child for example) which would require confession and repentance. Sometimes these transgressions happen in an unconscious or impulsive way, or sometimes because of a lack of self-control. In this case we have to understand that the process of civilization, as the Swiss psychiatric analyst Carl Gustav Jung said, requires a continuous domestication of the human "animal". Therefore sometimes this animalistic, impulsive, instinctive, aggressive and uncontrolled part of us emerges and generates these kind of acts, which with the passing of time and greater awareness can make people feel guilty. It is important to understand this dimension of our nature and if it does not cause much damage (ruin, death, abuse etc.) you have to be able to understand yourself, to tolerate yourself and to forgive yourself.

Atonement for some can be the path to purifying this guilt through a compensatory sacrifice. For example, someone who feels guilty for having offended their deceased father, or not having satisfied his expectations, can decide to compensate by becoming a professional in their field of work and by making an effort to reach excellence in honour of their father. We can understand this as a process of atonement. It can be said that when guilt stays trapped in an individual's psyche for a long time, they have to try to find a philosophical answer, a spiritual, impulsive, compensatory way out.

One way or another, depending on the person, we will find that in every one of these cases it is better to dilute this guilt. Sometimes this feeling is linked to a moment in childhood or in adolescence in which we did something "bad" and in adult age it has become an obsessive thought. For example it is very frequent between children or teenagers, sometimes of the same sex, for there to be erotic games where there is reciprocal touching. These belong to a phase of mutual exploration, a discovery of one's body and of what is different. Sometimes it happens with siblings or childhood friends. For the most part the people who have participated in these games, do not give it any importance as adults. It is considered nothing more than a mere anecdote. However, there are some who can become fixated on such events, on something that happened when they were seven or eight years old with a child of the same age. When they enter youth they begin to fixate on it as if they had been involved in some kind of perverse or malign way, and from there begins the path to obsession.

What is it that makes something like this unimportant to some people, and yet to others it becomes an obsessive thought? Evidently there is a genetic predisposition to a psychological vulnerability which consists of an overbearing domination of conscious reason over the basic impulses which reside in every human being. Instead of perceiving them as natural and common among human beings, it is judged through a moral filter. Here there is clearly a cognitive error, which needs to be diluted through some of the ways we have mentioned, through the activation of our drives but I repeat so as to be clear; neither genetic predisposition, nor moral rigidity alone, nor a singular event which happened in childhood, explains the appearance of an obsessive symptomatology. It is necessary for there to have been traumatic triggers of heightened anxiety: chronic stress in childhood/adolescence or a traumatic event during one of those periods.

g. Counting or organising things

Here we are on a different level of obsessive disorders. In the case of counting or organising things ritualistic thought or behaviour has been substituted for the conflictive content. The primary symptomatology of the neurotic conflict – such as a possible homosexuality or possible violence – is therefore concealed by a mental or behavioural compulsion.

The compulsion shows us a very high level of compressed anxiety, which runs the risk of bringing the affected person to an energetic paralysis. In this case the content of the obsession is placed aside and only the compulsion remains as a symptom.

When the mental rituals (adding, counting, remembering,...) or behavioural (tidying, cleaning,...) substitute for the obsessive content, we are faced with a high level of anxiety given that the person is completely trapped in a nervous blockage, and it will be more urgent in this case to return the person to *life*.

5. Is the content of obsessive thoughts important?

Yes, but never literally so. The content of obsessive thought is the weapon which the unconscious uses to force the affected individual to free themselves from the tyranny of the control exercised by their rational mind. The nature of the contents will therefore always be related to the blocked factors, but not in the same direction and nor in the same proportion in which the obsessions indicate. That means that the obsession with being homosexual indicates a repression of a masculine disposition, not from the sexual point of view, but from the daring point of view. The obsession with hurting others indicates a repression of aggression and this can apply in many other cases. For this reason we have to consider the content of the obsession, but in each case it is pivotal to know how to decipher its meaning, without succumbing to vain generalizations.

6. WHAT SHOULD A PERSON WHO SUFFERS FROM AN OBSESSIVE DISORDER DO?

Firstly they should take into account two fundamental factors. The first, which I mentioned before, is that while genetics predispose, they do not condemn. The second is that the human psyche is sufficiently flexible so as to cure itself, even in very serious cases. Organismic psychiatry considers that the disorder is chronic and the only thing that a person can do is to try to manage the obsessions and compulsions in the best way possible, learning rules and techniques for control and taking the corresponding medication. It is true that the medical protocol – a combination of specific anxiolytics and antidepressants, accompanied by behavioural therapy – has, from a statistical point of view, had the best results in most patients. In some cases it has stunted and reduced their symptomatology, but for the rest it has not made them better. But what I am proposing is a different focus, a focus fundamentally based on the activation and focalization of a person's drives. In addition to this, a personalized evaluation of the factors which triggered the anxiety in the first place is required, and then from there on we work out an effective way of reducing it.

A few ideas to start off:

I am going to give you some very simple pieces of advice, which will help people who have suffered in the shadow of this disorder for a long time, to see a little light, and above all to begin the work of diluting this anxiety.

a. Sport

Doing some kind of competitive sport will help. Here it is important to differentiate between two types of exercise. On one hand sports which do not require an excessive expression of impulses or instincts, for example going to the gym, swimming, cycling or jogging alone and on the other hand sports which are clearly competitive, where the person is "battling" with other people and against other people. The latter kind helps liberate and diffuse anxiety and repressed contents. For example, football, rugby, water polo, martial arts and especially boxing. In all these cases the person cannot be thinking about their repetitive thoughts while they are competing. In the former however it is possible for this to happen.

The best sports for a person with OCD are those in which you are unable to think, due to the fact that you have to be instinctively alert, and because they activate a certain level of aggression.

I especially recommend the four following sports:

- Boxing or Kickboxing: these are without a doubt the best sports for the type of disorder we are dealing with. Why? Because in order to practice these sports you need to confront your fear, your inhibition, especially if you have a coach who can guide you and train you to fight. There will come a moment when you will have to put yourself out there, to not only defend or shield yourself from your opponent's blows, you will also have to fight, and this will be the sign that a psychic change is taking place.

- Rugby: This sport requires a lot of animality. The French say that it is a dirty game played by gentlemen. This animality, unless you want to come across as a timid person standing in a field, will have to manifest itself, and this once again will represent a change.

- Paddle: this competitive sport on a closed pitch requires you to be quick and to use your reflexes. Therefore to play it well, you will have to come out of yourself.

- Horse riding: You will have to connect with the horse, otherwise it will get nervous. When horse riding you will develop calmness, security, inner strength, and finally control over yourself and over the animal. All of this will activate your psyche, will make it more daring and somewhat more savage.

- Rock climbing: When you reach a certain skill level and level of difficulty, you have to be very attentive and focus on your movements. This activates your boldness and determination.

It is very difficult to be thinking while practising one of those sports. On the other hand you can think while you swim, run or cycle. Do you understand the logic behind this?

All these sports should be practised – especially in the beginning – under strict supervision of a specialized professional.

b. Express what you think and feel

It is very normal for people who suffer from this disorder to find it very difficult to talk about their emotions and their thoughts. Sometimes out of fear, on other occasions because they are not used to doing so because of how they were brought up, because they are afraid of being mocked or reprimanded, etc.

There is a basic concept that I have already mentioned, which is that of assertiveness. Being assertive, fundamentally and synthetically, means saying what one thinks without offending others. For example, if I tell someone that they have said something inappropriate, that it annoyed me and I would prefer that they did not do it again, I am being assertive. If I hold it in, I am being a coward. If I tell this person that they are an idiot and that they should not talk to me anymore, I am being offensive. For this reason, the middle road, assertiveness, enables you to calmly advance through life, getting other people to respect you and giving definition to your personality, which luckily will never be perfect, nor to everyone's liking.

There is something we need to be crystal clear on: never, no matter how much we try, are we going to please everyone. There will always be people who sympathize with us, even forgive us for our terrible mistakes, but there will be others who are not so inclined and will anticipate and use any trifling matter to affirm the little chemistry they feel towards us.

Fundamentally, not understanding that as we get older, we must acquire life skills, develop our characters and a firm temperament while trying to hide them by adapting, in a chameleonic manner, to the different situations which present themselves. This may be considered unworthy, but it can also be seen as an act of pride. Trying to please everyone around you is an act of egomania. At the end of the day, we are nothing more than a small cog in the machinery of society and our surrounding ecosystem. Therefore, you simply should be yourself.

c. Arguing:

You should not be afraid of arguing. Even if it provokes anger and surprise from those who are used to seeing you being submissive. When faced with verbal aggression, a humiliation, contempt or an unfair criticism, the person who suffers from an obsessive disorder tends to remain silent, or to inhibit themselves. You need to get out of that position no matter what, unless you are afraid of physical violence because the other person is very aggressive. If this is not the case, you should never worry about powerfully expressing yourself. All things considered, even if this means you have to leave home until this person calms down, or shouts, or cries, it is necessary to do it.

Frequently, avoiding conflict is what has incurred such heightened levels of repression. This can go back years, and it will have forced the person into a state of mental prostration and obsessive energy.

d. Not accepting unjustified orders:

There are people who live under the authority of others who are capricious and authoritarian: despotic bosses or employees, dictatorial fathers, tyrannical spouses or any other possible combination we could make. It is absolutely necessary to know how to say no. Whatever happens, and at whatever cost. From that point on, what will happen needs to happen: leave fear behind.

Fear is an obsessive disorders biggest ally. If you are a coward, it will be much more difficult to overcome it.

e. Eroticism and Pleasure

Obsessive people often have great difficulty with pleasure and tend to convert sexuality into an unloading mechanism following traditional rituals and to reduce pleasure and eroticism, sometimes to a compulsive degree, to its most minimal expression. Searching for eroticism through one's body is a positive thing. It can be done by seeking out sensual experiences to be maximized into intense pleasure, without being merely "genital". The objective of this is not to reach orgasm but the sensual experience in and of itself.

You have to be mentally free to enjoy these experiences without becoming compulsive. Someone with an obsessive personality can penetrate or be penetrated many times and with/by many different lovers, but it is possible that there is little connection to the actual erotic experience for them. Their body has to be awoken, centimetre by centimetre, until it is capable of being freed from the controlling tyranny exercised by their rational mind.

f.   Breaking with moral rigidity:

In our lives there have to be ethical and moral pillars strong enough to prevent us from falling into compulsion, addiction or sensorial dilution. That said, when a person possesses a rigid morality, it is always hiding something dark, especially fear and anger, or sometimes some kind of perversion or inhibited rage.

I have never found people who are excessively moralistic to be trustworthy, apart from those who have developed a true spirituality based on faith and love. But this only applies to a minority of those I have encountered.

The majority of inflexible moralists are actually repressed. They are masked, even to themselves, because they are afraid of revealing themselves or rebelling against their conscience. Often they are also fearful, jealous and insecure. This makes them punish the sensorial impulses which they discover in others, and generate frustration when they see others who are less cowardly, enjoying life. They also feel a profound anger when faced with those who live freely and vigorously.

There is an American film which can serve as a perfect example of what I am describing: "American Beauty" (Sam Mendes, 1999). I recommend you watch it and see how appearances are deceiving.

Remember that moral inflexibility is against nature since it ignores true human needs.

g. Shouting/Screaming

I have recommended to some of my patients that they go to the mountain and shout. Shouting and screaming, much like weeping, is a magnificently liberating force. This only works on the condition that the shout is not theatrical and comes from deep down, surging upwards from deep within, and linked to a desire for freedom from a situation, a person, or some particular thought content. You have to scream until the soul is shaken, until all tension is emptied from your body. Shouting, above all, without fear, as if you were howling out to the universe that you are alive, present and actively taking part in the world.

You have to shout from your stomach, not from your throat, not least because you could become hoarse. You must take in air using your abdomen, and let the scream start from there and go up through to the throat. Shout and scream without the fear of being heard, without feeling ridiculous, without thinking of what they will say! Shout to free yourself, emit an animal noise, reaffirm yourself, position yourself forcefully in the world!

7. What should the family of someone suffering from an obsessive disorder do?

I receive many emails from young people who have been suffering from an obsessive disorder for a period of time, some for many years, and have yet to tell their families because they think that they will not understand. This is, in fact, frequently the case. Those affected by the disorder are not met with comprehension or they are simply not able to communicate in a clear way what is happening.

I have met parents who while in therapy with their children say such banal things as "you just need to distract yourself" or "what you need to do is sort yourself out and *stop thinking about stupid things*". If distracting yourself was so therapeutic as some seem to think, there would be no need for mental health specialists; as this piece of advice which consists of advising the patient to distract him or herself is one of the most commonly recommended by the members of the family of the sufferer.

The majority of the family members do not know that an obsessive disorder is one of the conditions which produces the most suffering. It contains reiterative thoughts, endless mental conflicts, compulsive fears and rituals which hardly leave any space for "life." A person can be trapped and thus brought to high levels of desperation and frustration; in some cases this leads to suicidal ideation. Further pressure is added when people affected by this disorder are asked or feel the need to explain themselves.

Imagine the fear of being a homosexual or a paedophile. Who do you turn to for advice? In some cases, with regards to the former, people have had the courage to tell someone. This may be thanks to their parents' comprehension, in the case of being young: "Well, don't worry, if you're gay we are still going to love you." In the case of the latter this never happens.

But this person is not even gay! They are just very repressed on a vital level and have developed anxiety!

Here I have to add that when I have a patient in front of me explaining me that he or she likes people from the same sex,- and this is not an obsessive thought but a reality, and therefore he doesn't have anxious doubts about the subject-, I work with them in order for them to completely integrate this into their sexual and their affective life. Moreover, I help them to accept it, dignify their life, and to become a completely integrated homosexual, both in themselves and in life.

For this very reason families must be very aware of the fact that someone with an obsessive fear needs to look for therapeutic help so that they can start a recovery process.

If the family or just one member of the family is capable of empathizing with the patient, they can represent a pillar of moral and affective support that provides a great deal of help until the person suffering finds a sufficiently valid method by which to be cured.

Please mind that if you are related to or friends with a person who has an obsessive disorder, that they are suffering a great deal. As I have already mentioned, I receive many emails (from young people to adults) from all over the world asking for help. For most of them it is the first time that they tell someone that they have these fears (which I have detailed previously) and just by feeling understood – I try to answer all of them – they feel a certain relief.

a. Family must be a space for affection and liberation.

Up until the appearance of express divorces and parental abandonment with their subsequent effects – due to a fundamentally misunderstood hedonism, an atrocious individualism, a lax teaching style in school, and radical feminism, which nearly denies the fact that there are biological differences between men and women, – for the majority of westerners the family was the structuring nucleus of an individual's personality. It was also the space where affection and defined limits permitted children to grow up in stable environments until they reached the age where they could become independent. Before, the roles in the majority of cases were clearly established. The mother was the principal dispenser of affection and care, while the father set the rules and taught the child to be daring. The trends over the last few decades have lessened the family and have left many people, the great majority, without solid structures which they can lean on. The role of the father is not undertaken by anyone anymore, by neither the mother, nor the father. Children tend to be raised by adults who possess an adolescent mentality. The lack of family stability which includes an absence of affection or contradictory messages can generate a psychic vulnerability, which in conditions of stress can cause someone to develop a psychological pathology.

b. A functional and structured family must be defined by five fundamental elements:

- Love: this is the maternal function and it must be present at the core of the family.

- Limits: this is the paternal function and it is important that these limits are applied.

- Self-esteem, responsibility and liberty: children need to grow up with a sense of self-esteem and security (not narcissism or arrogance). At the same time they must feel like their actions have consequences and that they are free to make their own decisions in the future.

- Individual autonomy of both parents. Do you think it's possible in the 21st century for a couple to be united for their entire life if they don't have a certain level of personal and private autonomy? Either we start using our heads and manage the *individual* needs of both adults that form the couple, or they will reach a point in which they collapse and this can easily lead to a break-up.

- Independence of parents with regards to their children: If parents, after their kids reach a certain age, renounce their own life by converting themselves into their slaves, it is possible they become resigned and dissatisfied, due to the fact that they are denying their own needs. In addition this doesn't bring anything good in the long run.

8. A BALANCED LIFE: THE PASSION TO LIVE

In our society, the majority of people are motivated by two types of interaction with reality: routine and distraction. Many of these individuals live immersed in routine processes which evidently help mental stability, including work days, sleep and meals, and beyond that most look for distraction. How do they do this? Usually in a very passive way, such as spending hours in front of the television, in front of computer screens, listening to music, or eating.

Therefore I posit this question: where is the passion? When passion is activated we awaken primary aspects in our being, because it means that an external or internal objective has generated such motivation that our biochemistry prepares itself to reach the objective. For example: a person we like, a profession or hobby we would like to do, a subject we would like to know more about, a trip we would like to make... When a life goal or objective generates passion within us, our whole organism becomes positively agitated. This takes us out of the inertia of routine and distraction. Most people who have an obsessive disorder lack passion. We cannot confuse passion with following a football or basketball team, because that is a passive activity, with anyone who is actively involved in the competitive sport (players, trainers, physiotherapists, presidents,...) and is acting and intervening in the process. We cannot consider any passive attitude to be passionate, because it does not activate our interactive or behavioural mechanisms in the process of reaching an objective.

Without passion there is no life and no high-points are reached and without active passion, there are no struggles to reach objectives. So either you channel your energy in pursuit of the goals you have set for yourself, or if there is an obsessive predisposition, it can start to present itself as a disorder.

I always give my patients two examples. Picasso dedicated his life to painting in a compulsive way. For example, he redid his famous painting *Les Demoiselles d'Avignon* many many times. His life was based on painting, on the games of love and sex and on his social relations. Can you imagine him working in an office? He would either burn down the office or he would generate an obsessive disorder. All that energy was brilliantly channelled into his painting, and chaotically, despotically into his relationships with women, as his biographers attest. Einstein, on the other hand, dedicated so much time to his research that for his wife to communicate with him she had to ask his permission through little hand-written notes which she would leave on his desk so that he could read them when he was able to. Were Picasso and Einstein two potential obsessive's? Or were they two people who were very passionate about their jobs? What would they have done with all that psychic and physical energy had they not been able to link it to their passions? Well, in the majority of those people affected by one or another kind of obsession, we find that when that energy is not connected to the outside world it becomes anxiety (since it goes around in circles and does not find a way out), which is the base of obsessive symptomatology.

I want to make something clear. Many patients, when I explain to them the concept of trapped energy, will turn to me and tell me that they do sport, they go out, they run, swim or go to the gym. I have to remind them that if the activity they practice does not create an emotional bond it will not help them to tackle an obsessive disorder. To be entirely clear, the only physical activities which can help you are those in which there is a high element of competition between the participants. What I mean is that it is only useful if someone is trying to win, independently of whether that is the end result or not (winning in this case is not important; what is important is giving it your all).

You need to be in connection with some intense emotions. Much like when you dance freely to music. That moment you almost reach a state of ecstasy and disconnect with the reality which surrounds you. In that moment you are forging a link between the physical and the mental, and for this reason you are working on your passion. When do we know that we are passionate about something? For me there is a clear indication, which is that when time flies, when we like something, when we are motivated and excited, we lose all concept of time. One of the secrets to having a balanced life is having elements of passion within it. Without this, where is the human component which differentiates us from animals? To paraphrase Stuart Mill in his essay "On Liberty", someone who only imitates in life does not need any more intellect than a monkey.

9. Tradition as the root but not as the future

Every human being needs to feel like they belong to a family, a community, a culture and a civilization. This will help them to create a strong mental structure and it will be absolutely necessary for their personal development. Feeling like you do not belong makes a person's development fragile, thus making them vulnerable from an emotional and psychological perspective. We can understand tradition as all those habits, customs, symbols and means of communication which form part of a certain culture. When tradition becomes a prison, because of a political dictatorship with fanatical ideologies for example, problems start to appear. They force individuals to live under a system which represses them on a personal level, many times causing social paralysis and economic decadence, to add to the generalized suffering of the population.

However, this is also the case in liberal western or western-style democracies (currently there are no other models for liberalism) where, for example, an individual can grow up in a very conservative family. In cases like these tradition becomes a stigma for their personal development. All tradition is linked to morals. Morality, sustained by different religions for millennia, has been the civilizing element which has domesticated the animal in the human being. The problem presents itself when this morality, as has been previously mentioned, becomes a prison for the individual. So tradition should be the starting point, but an individual must learn how to innovate, to experiment, to transgress if necessary. This is essential for anyone suffering from an obsessive disorder. If you are not able to free yourself from the shackles of tradition, in the case that they are so rigid that it prevents you from expressing yourself vitally, you will not be able to escape from the obsessive cycle. This means that at some point you will have to activate your "heroic side", something which is very difficult for most people who suffer from obsessions.

10. EXPERIMENTING, TRANSGRESSING,...

What do we mean by transgressing? Transgression, in the context of what we are working on, means being able to break from pre-established schemata. These schemata are normally based on three elements: 1) Fear of what they will say about me 2) Guilt 3) Sexual morality.

I once read a study by a British university, published in a newspaper in my hometown of Barcelona, which said that eccentrics tend to live longer, have better health and have more economic prosperity. Eccentrics are not necessarily extroverts, hysterical, or attention seekers. Put simply, they are people who do what they feel is right, without trying to offend or annoy anyone, without caring about the opinions of others.

Positive eccentricity, the kind which is not self-destructive, nor damaging to anyone, usually generates a lifestyle which is very satisfactory given that decisions are taken according to intelligence and desire, and the dependence upon other people's opinions is lessened.

11. Sexual morality

Human beings' sexual behaviour is configured by the morality which predominates at a given time and according to the society in which one lives. Basic human sexuality shows us that opposite sex attraction and coitus between sexes is "normal." I mean this in purely biological terms. However, from the moment that civilization appears, human sexuality becomes much more complex and experimental. This leads to many possibilities opening up and all types of interactions becoming possible between adults , according to how flexible and indulgent the laws and morality are where the person lives. In times of economic growth and social prosperity, sexuality opens up and individuals experiment with different kinds of interaction. In times of sobriety and austerity, which usually bring severe laws with them, sexuality becomes exclusively traditional. We cannot attribute the way someone lives their sexuality to solely the person, but also to the social-economic-political context (environmental) in which they find themselves.

This is why we have to absolve those who have sexual desires for people outside of their relationships. Behind all individual behaviour there is a biological reality and we can clearly say that more economic prosperity leads to more sexual freedom and vice versa. So it is very important to be aware that a person is not responsible for what they feel, because they are within a context. It is ridiculous that in the twenty-first century an individual can perceive his or herself as a whole and not as what they truly are, as a part of groups: part of a family, of a town or city, of a nation, of a culture, of a civilization, and part of a geo-biological and cosmological moment.

Personal freedom consists of managing your life well. We cannot help feeling impulses, we can only try to manage them. From our genetic nature through to the socio-political circumstances in which we have to live, we are conditioned. We can only guide ourselves with a level of tolerance and affection towards ourselves so that what we are can be expressed in the best way possible and without any great conflicts. You should never torture yourself for what you think about or feel on a sexual level. Whatever it is, you just have to deal with it in an ethical way, so that it can manifest itself in an adaptive way when confronted by the reality and society in which you live.

12. ROUTINE AND FEAR: TWO FORMS OF PARALYSIS

The majority of us live trapped in our compulsive consuming routines and compulsive need for distraction. These things modulate our lives, making us live between strict work hours and evasive entertainment through television or some other piece of electronic junk.

Aside from fear, the lack of boldness is a strong behavioural conditioner. As the saying goes, "most people hope that their circumstances will change, without changing one iota of their lifestyle." It is absurd to try to attain something without changing; the common strategy used by innumerable people. One day a friend of mine, a retired skydiver, said to me "if you're not afraid when you drop down with a parachute, you're not doing anything brave." Bravery is only shown in those things that make us scared. For me, for example, skydiving would represent a real test of bravery, since I have a certain phobia of heights and I feel a physical fear towards certain risks. However, it would not be a big problem for me to address an auditorium of two thousand people. For many other people it would be precisely the opposite. In my case overcoming fear would be by doing this sport, while for others it might be talking to a boy or girl they like, speaking in public, being capable of going against the wishes of their family, or daring to live in another country. These are all tests. Fear is something which the majority of obsessive patients feel when trying to stop established routines.

13. Inflexible thought vs. open thought:

I want to insist on this point.

Inflexible thought is characterized by basing yourself on limited parameters. A more colloquial term would be "staying in your comfort zone." In my office I have met patients who have felt bad simply for having ideas or dreams which went against their narrow moral code. For example, desiring people who were not their partner, having dreams in which they were participating in a violent act, homosexual fantasies, etc. I have already spoken about the difference between thoughts, dreams and behaviour.

One of the first things to accept if you suffer from an obsessive disorder is the need to free your thoughts, whatever they might be, and of course your dreams. Many times our desires or the things we repress appear symbolized in our oneiric production also known as our dreams. People with rigid thought patterns believe that there is only one way to be, to think and to do things, based on their traditions and what they've been taught. Evidently, in such variable times as ours, this kind of thinking can lead to economic and social failure and when it is prevailing, to pathology. Guiding yourself using highly traditional standards in times of globalization and social media, is to not understand that such times require being very open, an enriching of our own "software" so that we can adapt to the modern world. An excess of emotional independence, of attachment, of fanaticism, are indicators of low bio-social intelligence, and makes you at risk of remaining outside of the quick transformational processes which society generates.

Open thought should not be confused with the concept of "weak thought", formulated by the Italian essayist Gianni Vattimo. Weak thought refers to the relativism that is predominant in modern society. If inflexible thought considers that there is only one truth for every subject, then relativism, on the other hand, posits that everything is debatable. When everything is debatable all values become liquid, changeable, and instrumental, according to our own personal interests at any given moment. Weak thought can be as destabilizing and suffocating as inflexible thought, and taken to an extreme it could even become psychopathic. Given that it would leave the individual at the mercy of their whims and their impulses without any moral or ethical considerations. You need to find a balance with your thoughts in a way that you have clear ethical and moral values and by extension behaviour; but on the other hand not to be scandalized by what you see or what you think. This requires temperance and serenity, as well as having your sights set high when interpreting what you come across in the outside world, but also with what you come across from within.

With obsessive disorders it is very important that the person works on being able to develop open thought. You have to separate yourself from rigidity and relativism: **you have to have clear values but maintain an open mind**. Let us consider an example: imagine a heterosexual middle-aged couple. They have been together for ten years and have a good relationship. He likes painting and would like to paint the naked bodies of other women. Inflexible thought would consider this a moral transgression, even a kind of infidelity; by contrast open-mindedness would permit him to create this kind of artistic work.

Behind the fear of freedom many personal failures are hidden. Families and individuals who prosper, who maintain a considerable psychological and emotional equilibrium, are those who do not overly emotionalize or rationalize the facts, but instead confront change with intelligence and wisdom. Those who risk crossing stale traditional lines without succumbing to relativism or licentiousness. This balance is the challenge to take on for those who suffer from an obsessive disorder, since they have to learn to listen to themselves, to know their needs, and to be brave enough to integrate them into a new lifestyle. Several times I have met homosexual people who are incapable of integrating their orientation in an adequate way, living between the formal and inflexible appearance of a conservative world and the libertine impulse of casual sex, generating on many occasions a strong internal conflict.

The integration of who you are in all your facets, by getting to know yourself, by listening to and by feeling yourself is one of the most important things you have to do in order to overcome obsessive thoughts.

14. Pharmaceuticals, Alternative Medicine and Nutrition

a. **Pharmaceuticals:**

The pharmaceuticals which are usually prescribed for the treatment of an obsessive disorder are antidepressants and anxiolytics. These usually affect one of the aspects of the disorder more than the other (depending on the patient), those being depression or anxiety. Behind a disorder of this kind hides an intense anxiety fed by an unconscious fear, guilt and a sometimes unrecognizable depressive nucleus. For this very reason obsessive and compulsive thoughts can be a symptom of an incredibly high amount of anxiety, which in turn is activated by this depressive nucleus which has two basic components: desperation and fear. Behind these disorders there is a symbolic drowning, a sort of "downfall of the soul."

What would the downfall of the soul be? We can put it down to a lack of "erotic" connection with the world. This eroticism can be seen as those feelings of pleasure, of vitality and flow, which happen when we are receptive to external stimuli. When you're not connected to these anymore you have stopped living and just think. Normally this is due to, as we have mentioned previously, having suffered a traumatic experience, or having gone through adverse circumstances. These are the elements which, in a psychological sense, have caused this disconnect. It is a way of life defined by inertia, living without being alive, centred solely on a control of thoughts and actions which impede a more genuine vital expression. Therefore these pharmaceuticals at a biochemical level try to regulate these symptoms. What happens for some people is that everything is so knotted up that medication is not enough because this unconscious nucleus, which continually generates a serious state of anxiety, is so dense.

Organismic psychiatrists consider that much like other disorders, obsessive disorders have a structural component and that you have to learn to live with it. For this very reason, it is considered that the combination of medication with cognitive-behavioural therapy is an adequate path to functioning more or less properly. However, in many cases when this kind of treatment is applied the suffering is still the same or only slightly reduced. I want to be completely clear that I am in favour of the use of pharmaceuticals when they are necessary to reduce the level of suffering the person is experiencing; I am also the first to recommend seeing a psychiatrist so that the patient can be prescribed said medication to be taken in conjunction with the therapeutic process which the patient will undertake with me.

Contrary to these organismic ideas, my therapeutic experience has shown me that some cases which were considered chronic have been completely cured or reduced to insignificant levels of obsession. This in turn reaffirms my theory that yes, a genetic predisposition or a vulnerability can exist, but this is not a structural condition on an organic level. There have been cases of people who had spent years suffering from a very serious case of obsessive compulsive disorder and who have been able to overcome it. Their personality will always tend to be obsessive, but only in a normative sense.

I do not wish to question other people's therapeutic paths but I can say this without a doubt: if you do not reduce the anxiety and unblock the depressive knot through intensive and deep therapy to unpick the origins – and this requires an eclectic and humanist profile – there is no point in learning how to deal with the thoughts.

To sum up, pharmaceuticals are useful, but only when combined with the adequate therapeutic process which removes the psychic and physical bases which generate this symptomatology, as well as a progressive diminution, monitored by a psychiatrist as the therapy start to give positive results.

b. **Nutrition:**

If at the base of an OCD there is anxiety, it is evident that you should not be ingesting any type of stimulant, such as coffee, tea, cola, energy drinks or chocolate. You should also switch meat protein for vegetable protein. To someone who is suffering psychologically, this may seem anecdotal, but I have observed in some patients a slight improvement just by stopping their consumption of sodas. You have to be vigilant with your diet so as to make sure that it not only does not increase anxiety, but that it may even reduce it. No one will be cured by stopping drinking coffee, but by doing so you may notice a slight reduction in the symptoms.

Reducing sugar intake is also something which should be considered.

c. **Natural Remedies:**

When prescribed by a naturopath or doctor specialized in such matters, tryptophan, St John's Wort, balm mint or maypop are natural remedies which have a low amount of therapeutic effect compared to other pharmaceuticals, but are sufficiently valid to be used in combination with therapy. This is only applicable in milder cases.

15. Meditation, Mindfulness and Breathing:

I learned how to meditate when I was twenty-five and went on a fifteen day getaway on the island of Ibiza with some nomadic Buddhist monks who had travelled around the world. I spent fifteen days living in a quasi-monastic way, with vegetarian food, sexual abstinence, regulated sleeping hours and eight hours of meditation a day spread out in four blocks of two hours throughout the day. I can say without a doubt that this experience was a turning point in my life and changed it to the extent that there was a before and an after. I will not go into too much detail, but what happened to me there is linked to what the master monk later recognized as the awakening of Kundalini. What surprised me and what I recommend my patients is the simple meditation technique which they taught us.

Firstly, you can do it lying down or sitting comfortably with your eyes closed, so it did not require special training, even though the monks were sitting in the lotus position. I, much like the majority of the neophytes who took part, did it by lying down on a mat on the ground. It consisted of creating a mantra of two words, for example "love and peace" or "truth and serenity" or "freedom and calm." It did not matter what the words were as long as they were positive and benevolent concepts chosen by each participant. In a sense, the objective was to "tame the mind." We had to mentally repeat these two words non-stop, without trying to visualize anything, and every time our thoughts would err into other topics we would have to try to gather up our thoughts and centre ourselves on those two words. During the first sessions you can err up to every three seconds and it can feel like taming a wild horse. It can seem almost impossible, but after a little time you become more and more centred on the internal repetition of your mantra and as you build up your mastering of the mind the feelings of pleasure and serenity are very high. I recommend all my patients and to those readers affected by this obsessive disorder to do at least thirty minutes of meditation a day. Those who do practice it eventually find a state of serenity which of course helps to dilute the anxiety and therefore also the obsessive component. I would like to add that for those who suffer from this disorder in the beginning it will be very difficult to "tame" the mind, but with perseverance and consistency you can do it.

<u>Mindfulness</u>

This technique is inspired from meditation, though without its spiritual component. Here the objective is to live in the moment, the here and now, concentrating on the "present moment." This technique is spreading more and more given that it is showing itself to be effective in the reduction of anxiety and stress.

Its practice is a highly beneficial addition to the treatment of obsessive disorders.

<u>Breathing</u>

There is a breathing technique which consists of lying down on your back and breathing in through the mouth, filling the abdomen and breathing out through the mouth, all for approximately fifteen minutes, with your eyes closed. Your mouth has to be kept open as if it was the beginning of a tube.

This breathing makes you hyperventilate slightly, which forces more oxygen into the blood, and therefore makes oxygen penetrate the internal layers of your musculature, liberating the molecules which compact them when you have a lot of internal nervous tension, which is often chronic.

Normally the areas where there will be a slight tingling sensation will be the feet, the hands, the mouth, and in some people the abdomen or the chest. Others will not notice anything, but even then it is a still an effective way to reduce nervous tension. You can do this, three times a day for example, fifteen minutes at a time. You should however never do this directly after eating. There are several precautions which should be taken in each case, for example those who have imbalanced arterial tension, who suffer from heart problems, or who have had a psychotic episode should be prudent and contact their doctor before undertaking this activity. This breathing done frequently can help to unblock all of the organism, which in the case of obsessive disorders is inflexible and prone to spasms.

16. THE ROLE OF THE THERAPIST:

One day in the future, which I hope will not be too far off, it will be proven that a patient can only be cured if the therapist, not being affected by a bloating of their ego, believes that they can help to cure and feels sufficiently motivated so as to be truly implicated in the healing process.

This means that all healing is an affective process in which the "Eros" (in this case the chemistry and alchemy between two people) must be activated. Converting countertransference – which in a nutshell means the unconscious feelings for the patient felt by the therapist – into something aseptic and neutral, is condemning the therapy to failure and to an excessive duration and inefficiency.

In the case of obsessive disorders there should never be any treatments in which the therapist is not able to link his or herself to the patient or potentiate archetypes within. An example of such an archetype is the "hurt healer"; this is a person who has experienced emotional pain under particular circumstances in their life and this makes them able to empathize with their patients.

I would like to add something politically incorrect: this does not apply for all. There may be patients who are insignificant to the therapist, patients who generate a negative countertransference or for whom the therapist feels indifference given the lack of real connection between them. Therefore there is a problem, because the nature of this connection can be varied but they – patient and therapist – must have a genuine therapeutic connection. Should this not be the case, the most honest thing to do would be to redirect that person to another therapist or transform the situation until it is possible to have an authentic connection. The work undertaken with a person who has a serious obsessive disorder requires much more than a purely rational and logical position.

17. INDEPENDENCE: AN IMPORTANT FACTOR IN OVERCOMING AN OBSESSIVE DISORDER

As I have explained throughout this book, what generates an obsessive disorder is the heightened level of anxiety activated by a blockage which appeared due to a traumatic, stressful episode or a chronic situation at some point during childhood or adolescence. This trauma could be the case of a boy or a girl who suffered sexual abuse or a dramatic one-off situation. On the other hand a chronic situation happens when ¡a child or a teenager lives with a heightened psychological tension over a prolonged period of time. It could be for example parents continually arguing accompanied by occasional explicit or veiled threats. Both traumatic and chronic situations can cause a nucleus of anxiety to get ingrained in the brain. This nucleus is therefore the most important factor when treating an obsessive disorder. But we have to take into account cognitive aspects as well and among them an important one is independence.

Normally, the majority of people are used to thinking within certain parameters, in such a way that their reflections always happen within those said parameters and never go beyond them. This is why, even if you read a million self-help books, if you do not manage to break and overstep those limits, you will not be able to change anything.

To explain this a bit better I will use an example: imagine I am in a room of an apartment with another person and I tell them that I have lost my pen. I ask them to help me find it. We both start to look in different areas of the room, but neither of us finds anything. Until one of us thinks "it is possible that it is outside this room." Here the room would represent the cognitive territory within which you are used to navigating. Outside this room would be unknown territory where you could, possibly, find the answer or the solution to a problem.

I have already mentioned my love of detective novels, a large part of which play on the idea of isolation. The writer knows how to direct the reader's attention to those people or situations which make it impossible for them to see the bigger picture. One of the most common tricks used is to make the reader think that the answer is so obvious that they think it is simply not the case, since the writer knows that those who read these books like to play detective themselves. The writer hides the murderer in full and clear sight, so obvious that the reader will dismiss their presence as far too simple. Edgar Allan Poe, in his short story entitled "The Purloined Letter", makes everyone look desperately for a letter, which no one can find. In fact it is in the most obvious place for a letter: in the card rack which is visible to everyone. So in a sense a way to hide something from someone is to make it visible.

The great marketing experts know how to make people who go into their malls buy something, by for example going through a great deal of aisles before getting to the till. The distribution of products, the lights and the sounds will guide the person through a whole process and in a high percentage of cases they will leave with more products than they had intended on buying. Those very same experts who work for big corporations can place us within a social group and predict ten or fifteen years in advance what we will be buying. What does this mean? That isolation is not a factor which is often considered.

This really is a question of intelligence. It requires training to think differently than the majority of the population. There are moral prejudices, that is to say, that within each of our imaginations there exists an idea of what is wrong and what is right and to add to that we all have this feeling that if we do not do the correct thing we will be judged by our entourage, society, friends and family. This condemns the majority of individuals to non-evolution, because there are so few who dare to transgress the limits which are considered the norm. It is very likely that as you read that last sentence, you associated the word "transgress" with something sexual, when in fact most of these transgressions are done by many people and do not make people evolve, nor even could we say it is related to the concept of isolation.

The transgressions I refer to are all those which require bravery, as when we do something which scares us.

Imagine a father who dedicates all his weekdays to work and the weekend to his children, taking them to different places. Realizing he has little or no time for himself he decides one day to turn his life around, but he wants to do this without abandoning his family. What could he do? For most people the most immediate response would be to find a hobby, however that means being a slave to a hobby. Are there other options? Isolation is necessary so as to find the correct answers, and some manage it. We can find many examples of isolation in the biographies of people who have done extraordinary things, and in many cases we will find that none of them violated an ethical principle. They simply were able to differentiate the primary from the secondary and they never gave the letter a minute of thought.

Not long ago I read W. Dyer's book, "Think Different, Feel Different." Dyer does not discover anything particularly new in his latest book, but his work continues to be vital and positive since it helps you to focus your life on optimism and pragmatism. In this book the author admits to not feeling the need to attend family events, be they with his own children or those of his grandchildren. As a father of the family he was therefore spared birthdays, anniversaries, and other family events. Since all were previously announced, no one could take it personally. Do you realise the amount of time which this man has given himself and the freedom it permits him? This does not mean he was not a family man anymore. But he became a family man in a way that was sustainable to him.

Federico Fellini, the famous Italian film director, while he was in Rome supposedly studying law, financed by his parents from Rimini, dedicated his time to painting on the windows of bars the products they sold. With the money he made and received from his parents he made comics, which permitted him subsequently to work for an editorial. He did not have any regrets for not studying what he was meant to because his vocation in the world of image creation was so great that it did not create inner conflict. Fellini was not doing anything which would have converted him into a parasite, he was instead doing something which he was passionate about and which his parents would not have wanted nor accepted for him. We all know the result: one of the most brilliant directors ever to have existed, with an uncountable amount of awards and international hits to his name. Let us go back to what we were discussing previously; why do almost one hundred per cent of those who suffer from an obsessive disorder lack this capacity to isolate themselves? Why do they find it so difficult to consider life outside common standards and considerations? Why do they feel obliged to do what they think that they should do? Is there a predisposition for this? As the French psychoanalyst Erich Fromm would have said "we are dealing here with a profound fear of freedom." Consequently for most of these people, activating this capacity to isolate is something which will help them better their lives. Firstly they will personalize them for themselves, secondly they will find alternative answers to old questions, and thirdly they will introduce elements of originality. In the case of people who suffer from depression this is absolutely necessary, because the field within which they move is too narrow and rigid.

How do you activate the capacity to become more independent?

- Reading biographies.

- Analyzing the behaviour of those who act differently to the majority (instead of criticizing them).

- Asking yourself how many unnecessary things you do that you do not like.

- Questioning the kind of relationships you have with other people, if they are satisfactory for you, or if they are simply based on routine and submission.

- Adopting new perspectives and new lifestyles. Or travelling (for those who can afford to do so).

- Introducing art and culture in all its dimensions into your life.

- Practising empathy and putting yourself in the shoes of others, including those who think or feel differently than you.

18. Dionysian activation

This is possibly the most important chapter of this book. Here, the real secret to the healing process is enclosed and explained. My training as a Jungian analyst has made me able to explore the world of the pagan gods, their hidden symbology and the power of being able to express yourself through your unconscious.

I can state without a doubt that if you do not integrate Dionysus there is no cure.

Dionysus was one of the Greek deities, son of Zeus, king of the gods, and Semele, a mortal woman.

Dionysus, masculine and feminine, represents the ecstasy which comes through music, the arts and wine, essentially when we give up control of our actions and we give ourselves up to sensorial experiences. He is the psychic compensation for his brother Apollo, symbol of order, logos, rationality and structure.

Dionysus is present in parties, in sex when it is experienced freely and pleasurably, in the laughter of a group of friends having a glass of wine, in the poetry which lifts the soul, in the watching of a film which fills us with enthusiasm, in a massage which is given or received sensually, in swimming in the moonlit sea, in the music which makes us dance and sing, in the game of seduction, in the body when it relaxes, feels and frees itself.

So now I ask those of you who are suffering from an obsessive disorder to activate the "Dionysian" in your life. How would you do it? It's hard, isn't it? Do you know why it is so difficult for you? Because you are trapped within your logos, in your thoughts, in control, because the anxiety generates repetitive thought loops, interminable conflicts, permanent checking up on things or obligatory rituals.

So how do you activate Dionysus?

Before answering this question, I have to remind readers that the process of integrating "the Dionysian" requires the same perseverance as when you learn how to swim. You cannot just go one day to the swimming pool, do what the instructor asks, get scared and not return for three months. That way you will never learn. This is not a bad example, because the "Dionysian" in obsessive personalities produces terror and usually generates a posteriori remorse since you "enjoy it" or you "get pleasure from it" and in many cases with obsessive people this can generate an inner conflict.

So let us activate it:

- Dance: at home, alone, put on music and let loose, throw yourself on the ground, jumping crazily, try to live this experience even if you feel ridiculous, try and enjoy it.

- Getting a sensual massage: not therapeutic ones, but ones which produce real sensorial pleasure. This does not mean that the massages have to be sexual in nature, they have to be sensually done and experienced. And the person who gives it to you has to be someone you find attractive, be it your partner, your friend or a professional. It is very important to be honest with yourself. It does not matter if you are young or old, if you have a partner or not, you need to find someone who will take you to the point of the dissolution of your senses, where relaxation and pleasure become one. I insist that there is no need for there to be anything sexual involved. Of course it would be a different matter if you wanted to add it.

- Drinking and eating: try to take your time when preparing food you like, and if you can, and you can withstand it, drink in moderation. You should do this until you reach a point where you feel yourself become uninhibited. Make food and drink a sensual experience too. Learn how to make elaborate and exquisite dishes and above all learn how to cook alone.

- Express yourself creatively: paint, write, sculpt, do ceramics, play or compose music, do landscape, urban or nude photography for example.

- Free your body: go to nudist beaches, saunas and steam rooms, share nudity with other people. Delight yourself in your shapes and those of others.

- Hug and maintain affectionate contact: but only with those you want to do that with. Do not force yourself to hug someone for whom you feel nothing or someone who disgusts or repels you. But when you feel it, either through friendship, physical attraction, fraternity, familiarity, or love, get closer, hug and try to be mindful of the reaction of the other person, whether they hug you back or reject you. It does not matter, in these cases you have to know how to *flow*, and there are always people around us who we enjoy hugging.

- Read: reading generates pleasure when you find the kind of texts that you like. I recommend, much more than a self-help book, to read novels and biographies. They are much more weighted in truth, emotions and experiences. The majority of those who devour self-help books never change anything. They generally are people who know all they should know about how to transform their lives, but because they have not managed to emotionally connect it nor "wake up their conscience" they are left with the same routine as always but with slightly more independence, which means very little.

- Fall in love: we should fall in love every five years either with our lovers or third parties. This does not mean that you need to break continually with what you have because loving is much more than being in love. Life however can end up becoming rather boring and you have to know how to inject new emotions into your life, without throwing the baby out with the bathwater. Life is a game and you need to know how to play. You should not live like a monk or a nun, nor like a bull in a china shop so that every time something is moved there is an emotional tsunami.

- Transgress: transgression has two limits, the law and ethics. Both of these must be respected but from now on, and if this does not put you in danger, you should try to be more driven, to be more radical, to break with the established limits of what is correct or incorrect which has enslaved you until today.

- Travel: nowadays many people travel but few people vibrate when they do. I have always found the people who photograph everything non-stop to be very stupid. When are they going to see these photos again? Or worse, who are they going to torture by showing and explaining each photo? Is this really travelling? I believe that there are those who do not look at anything save through the lens of a camera. Please try and live your trip! Let yourself be seduced! Experience it!

- Break out of the routine and boredom: do what you need to do but get out of your current position in life since all you are doing is fomenting obsession and mental slavery. Find new people, new circles of friends, new situations, create a problem situation which is sufficiently intense (always within the parameters of the law and ethics) so that it liberates you from your current life. Sometimes the only way to escape a "mental prison" is to break the bars holding your bravery in, there are no more conditions.

I could write many more examples, but with these you can get a vague idea of what you can do. I understand that for many conservatives this seems frivolous, to others impossible. Many others will simply not know where to start, but this is key to the therapeutic process and one of the aspects I work on most when trying to free my patients from obsessive disorders. You have to bring them back to life and use all the necessary resources that it can offer. This works.

19. WHY CAN AN OBSESSIVE DISORDER BE CURED?

Contrary to the prevailing belief held by Organismic psychiatrists and cognitive-behavioural psychologists, an obsessive disorder can be cured. I have mentioned in a previous section that there is indeed a genetic predisposition which makes some people more vulnerable to certain illnesses. But the vulnerability, I repeat, does not condemn: it only predisposes you to develop the illness.

I had not even thought about promoting my method or even writing this book, until I had confirmed the complete healing of a minimum threshold of patients who had suffered from this disorder at a considerably serious level. I feel that due to this I am legitimized to say that this disorder can be healed in a high percentage of cases.

When you say that the human psyche and the human body are in constant interaction, that they form part of the same unit, and on the other hand that our genome can be modified by external factors. That in reality we are nothing more than a wavelength, that we are in continuous transformation, from that moment on nothing can be considered hermetic, unchangeable, or permanent. Unless someone with academic authority considers it so and so it becomes engraved in our minds, in such a way that it becomes an absolute truth which structures many important parts of our lives. If a doctor tells a person who is living in despair that they will never be healed and that they have to therefore learn how to live with this condition, it can be very difficult for that person to overcome it, now that a strong psychological imprint has been left in the psyche of the individual.

For this reason the principal factor for me was that nothing is immovable. The possibility for change under any circumstances therefore is logically very high. I understood that a patient with an obsessive disorder is a living being trapped in his or her own prison. A prison from which no matter how much you may wish and try to free yourself, the walls will become narrower. The most common solution was to give pills so as to be able to live within the confines of this internal prison and teach the person to accept living in it without further upsetting themselves.

But what is it that has stopped them being free? The answer: anxiogenic experiences. These are those events and happenings which over the long-term generated a cumulative heightened degree of anxiety. My idea was, if we are able to dissolve them, we can free the person from the disorder.

20. A FAIRYTALE AS A SYMBOL:

I will now explain to you a story, of my own creation, with which I would like to exemplify what happens during an obsessive disorder and how you can overcome it. I was inspired by the classic narrations of the Germanic fairy tale tradition:

"Many, many years ago, in a land far away, and, a boy was born whose destiny it was to become a prince. His father, the king, was a man with a very severe, authoritarian and rigid character. His mother, the queen, submitted to the whims of her husband's temperament. The prince was born smiling, and the people of the palace were all surprised at his tendency towards happiness, something which his father could not stand. The child grew and grew and his happy and lively character was a pleasure for all the residents of the palace, especially his mother, to see. But the king could not abide this placid existence which was so far away from what he was and had been. When the future prince celebrated his fifth birthday his father called for him. Once before him, as if his son were an adult, the future prince was placed in front of his father and his father said to him: "You are the reason for my unhappiness. Since you were born I have not been able to sleep. From now on you are responsible for all my dissatisfaction."

The child barely understood a thing, and though he had been scared, he continued to play, to laugh as always. This embittered the king, and his anger turned itself into hatred for his son. A little later, he once again summoned his son to him and ordered him to paint an empty room in the palace. Three supervisors were charged with overseeing day after day the young prince's work. It was a massive room from which he could only leave to eat and to sleep. The child was more and more saddened by the punishment, for which he was not aware of deserving, but despite all this, he showed himself to be a happy and generous child. His mother, the queen, suffered inconsolably for the injustice which her son was being subjected to, but the king was an unscrupulous tyrant capable of making any situation a cruel and painful one. In fact, he only allowed her to see her son a few minutes a day.

The child was once again called before his father's throne and the king confirmed that there were still elements of happiness within his son's temperament. Angered, he ordered for this son to be locked in the room which he had been painting. Now he could not leave, neither by day nor night. The mother could only visit him behind the bars in the door. Soon after the king prohibited all visits by the prince's mother altogether.

The child grew up and became a teenager. Within this room and with almost nothing to do, he walked around in circles, drawing on the walls, and thinking in ideas which eventually became repetitive because of the lack of elements stimulating his imagination and of the total lack of freedom. The teenager grew and became a handsome prince. At one point his desperation almost became too much and he shouted into the night. During the day he hit the walls and the bars, but nothing came of it, everything stayed exactly the same. He did not receive a single visit, and his mother was prohibited to get close to him under the threat of punishing the prince with death. Only a lackey was allowed to bring him food and very few words were exchanged. The sadness of the prince and his desperation consumed all his energy and he spent most of his time lying on the floor, with hardly the strength to move.

The despairing mother did not know what to do. One day as she wept while sitting on her bed, a noblewoman approached her and said to her: "Your majesty, your pain moves me and I would like to give you a piece of advice if I may." The queen took a hold of herself and since it was a woman she trusted, she answered her: "Speak. But I hope that your words will console my heart since the pain has me at the threshold of death." The woman continued: "There has been talk of a wise man who lives in a nearby kingdom who has managed to soften the heart of many a man hardened by life. If you would like, I could bring him to our court." The queen answered immediately and annoyed asked "Do you think that he could free my son?" "That I do not know, your Majesty," said the noblewoman, "but I think it might be worth you seeing him."

Everything was put into motion. After a few days the sage had a private meeting arranged in the queen's quarters. Of course the king had no idea what was going on. It would be considered almost a crime of high treason to consult someone from outside the court without his prior permission. Stealthily, the wise man entered through a secret door of the palace accompanied by the queen's private secretary. The noblewoman was waiting for him and accompanied him to the room where he was to be heard.

He was an old man of short height, with a white beard and a comprehensive look. Upon seeing him the queen asked him to come near. When she was about to speak to him, he interrupted her, and since he had been informed of the drama which was happening he said: "Your Majesty, you should offer a sacrifice so that your son may be freed." The queen, ready and alert, firmly answered yes . She was prepared to do anything.

What was it that she needed to do? The wise man cleared her doubts: "you will have to offer your life." Loving mother that she was, this did not cause her any problems to accept. The only thing she wanted to make sure of was that her death would not be in vain; that is to say that her son be freed, since that if she died there would be no one to take care of the prince anymore. The wise man said: "Your Majesty, I have not asked you to sacrifice yourself, but to put your life at risk." "What do I need to do?" she asked. "Confront your husband," he answered, "but you have to do it front of the whole court. I will be among the courtesans, and when the opportune moment presents itself I will intervene so that your life should not be in danger. I do not know if I will be successful in this endeavour but I shall try."

The queen agreed to this and one week later there was the celebration of the king's jubilee. The king, as has already been said, was a tyrannical and capricious person. The court and the people were afraid of him. He had been incapable of being happy; his disposition towards jealousy and resentment made it impossible for him to value any positive aspects of existence. Many had been condemned to death, or imprisoned, much like his son. Confronting him could have disastrous consequences, not just for the queen, but for the whole country. The wise man refused to give even the tiniest detail of what his plan entailed.

The royal hall, where the most important events were celebrated, could hold a thousand people: all the members of the court and the king's most important subjects, as well as members from the royal households of neighbouring countries. Everything was prepared with such detailed and exquisite luxury. There was an abundance of delicacies and musicians enlivened the proceedings before the arrival of the king. Suddenly the trumpets sounded and the king, with the queen at his arm, appeared nearing the central aisle towards the two thrones which symbolized their power. The queen trembled, she was sweating, she knew that the most difficult moment of her life was about to begin. The freedom of her son compelled her to put her life at risk.

As they sat and the hall fell into silence, the king stood up to say a few words. "Ladies and gentlemen," he said, "I want to thank you for coming to this celebration which commemorates the thirty years of happiness and prosperity which I have given you." Suddenly, as if possessed by some unknown spirit, the queen rose to her feet and shouted: "No!" Her shout reverberated along the walls. It was followed by an absolute silence. The king turned around and looked at her with hate in his eyes, with a soul bent on destruction. She was terrified, but gaining strength from her weakness, she went on screaming "no!" louder and louder. The "nos" came from her soul, from deep inside her gut. The king was beside himself, he did not know how to react. Nobody dared to move until he gave the order, and suddenly he shouted: "Detain her." Three soldiers situated on the other side of the great hall, ran with their swords towards the queen. The queen continued shouting "no, no, no" and her shouts moved even the coldest of hearts.

All of a sudden, a spear flew across the hall from the opposite corner and hit the king straight in his forehead. The king collapsed to the floor without losing that look of bitterness which had always accompanied him. The subjects and the guests, unmoved and impassive, did not know what to do. The queen had three seconds to react. Those instants marked the future of the country. She could not make any mistakes. She became firm, lifted her head, turned to her assistants and said in a high, secure and emphatic voice: "I am the queen." Neither her voice nor her pulse trembled.

During a brief moment which felt like an eternity, nobody reacted. But little by little the assistants started bowing their heads one by one, until the whole hall was prostrate before the majestic figure of the new monarch. They were all conscious of the liberation which this act represented, but none dared to make the slightest comment or movement. Meanwhile, silently and discreetly, the small man with the white beard and slight aspect gradually disappeared from view as he made his way towards the exit. Nothing else was ever heard of him.

The queen, now invested with all her powers, liberated the prince, to whom she had for five years taught how to be sure of himself, rebellious and free before others. She did not give him the crown until she was convinced that he would make a good king, a balanced and mature man, in whom resided kindness, firmness, resolution, a sense of justice, compassion and the capacity to bear arms if necessary. Once she was certain that he was a real man, she abdicated to dedicate herself to meditation, to writing stories and narrations for the future generations inhabiting the country.

The prince, upon becoming king, reigned for many years up until his death . He remembered at all times of his life, that no matter what the price, and even at the peril of losing your life, you should never submit to the tyranny of an insecure and bitter despot.

What do the different characters represent?

- The king: in this case he is an authoritarian figure, rigid and incapable of being happy, he hates freedom and spontaneity. We are dealing here with a tyrannical, mannered, insecure logos who dominates through fear. It is the representation of dictatorial reasoning. (Obsessive thought).

- The prince: he represents freedom, spontaneity, happiness. He is our innate, free nature, which is connected to life. (Original nature).

- The queen: she represents the most primary drives: love, the capacity to overcome your own fears, and being daring. (Primary drives).

- The wise man: he represents the knowledge which you can re-establish, through the activation of our drives, our original nature, free from obsessions. (the role of therapy).

- The prison: this represents the obsessive disorder, the internal prison from which we must escape.

- The spear: it is the weapon which is activated thanks to the primary drives (the shouting of the queen) and ends up killing the tyranny of controlling thought (the king).

It is a simple story but sufficiently graphic so as to be able to understand the different elements which participate in the creative process and in freeing yourself from an obsessive disorder.

21. WHAT IS MY METHOD FOR CURING AN OBSESSIVE DISORDER?

To explain my method it is necessary to understand the fundamental premises of my theory about obsessive disorders. It is one in which an obsessive disorder is caused by an excess of accumulated anxiety over the years in the patient's physical organism. I distinguish the physical from the mental, because the psyche will become symptomatic of the physical blockage. Therefore and as a necessity we will have to firstly liberate ourselves on a physical level so as to after restructure the content and the way the patient focuses their life.

This method is quite different to what is usually done and practiced. Usually what is done is that a mixture of pharmaceutical anxiolytics and antidepressants are prescribed accompanied by cognitive-behavioural therapy. The reason for there being cases of people who after years of treatment with no results have been completely cured is due to the logic behind this therapy, which is completely different, and though it may seem strange to say, simpler.

Imagine a tiger locked in a fifty square meter cage. This cage may seem spacious, but not for a tiger. The animal will wander nervously from one place to another looking for a possible exit. Its carers will give it food and drink, they will clean its cage, but the tiger will become more aggressive and more nervous. This is why they will decide to give him the adequate medication so that it may become passive and withstand being locked in. After that a trainer will come and will show it how to do different exercises within the cage. Both of these will calm him down temporarily, but the tiger went through critical moments, where he was even capable of harming himself, itself, where he prostrated himself, itself, where he it tried to hurt others, etc. Can you think of a way to stop the tiger from suffering? It is very simple: by freeing him it. but now we have to try to imagine that we are freeing him after ten years of being locked up, and suddenly we discover that even while he is free to roam, he still more or less has the same habits and attitudes: he remains aggressive, keeps on walking in a small habitat and hardly explores the positive terrain.

This is exactly what happens with people who suffer from OCD. For this reason, it is not helpful to teach people how to live, resigning them to a fate which no one wants. Basically telling them to live in a cage, while administering them medication so that they may do that (this does not mean, as has been said before, that they are not necessary in the first phase of the treatment I use). This simply does not work. Neither is it useful to teach someone to live without having freed them previously from all the blockage on an instinctual level which this kind of imprisonment causes.

If humans were tigers, what I would propose on a therapeutic level would be to awaken again within them all those instincts which have been lost: explore, hunt, protect, recognize your peers, play, fight, mark your territory, establish hierarchies, etc. Since we are humans, and we supposedly live in civilized society, we have to rekindle those instincts in an artificial way, combining them where possible with real day-to-day life experiences.

Now, let us continue with the example of the tiger. Imagine that his joints after ten years of living inside a cage have lost their flexibility. He might have even developed some kind of pathology at a cardiac level which makes training, for an untamed life, difficult. We would need to do something previously. Maybe we have to cure only up to where we can and be conscious of those limits. With people who have obsessive disorders something similar happens: awaking instincts, drives, freeing emotions such as anger and fury, resentment, the need for affection, requires care and work on the body and the mind. We are talking about a progression in treatment which takes you from a direct unblocking of the body, of the anxiety which has materialised somatically in certain parts, to fostering the eruption of vital forces from your personality, the contents of your thoughts, as well as nurturing character and a temperament strong enough to withstand time and not relapse.

These would be the steps: First, try to understand the circumstance or circumstances which led to the generation of the high levels of anxiety which ended up as reiterating obsessions. Second, detect the structure of the patient's personality, and if necessary, start working on the content of the obsessive thoughts. Third, physical unblocking. Fourth, the liberation of instinct, drive and emotions. Five, the restructuring of beliefs. Six, the search for the patient's main archetype: who is it? What myth explains their life? Once the treatment has been finalized, the patient must be free of the obsessive disorder and at the same time have a clear focus on the route they must follow in life. This focus will not based on judgements, *a priori*, but based on the work on a profound level of the unconscious which will supply emerging content and allow the harnessing of the energy which was blocked before.

22. Many patients: many cures

In the past few years I have received many enquiries and requests for therapy from all parts of the world, for this reason the professionals who work in my center in Barcelona provide therapy in several languages: principally in English, Spanish, Italian, Dutch and French. The international demand for AFOP® is constantly growing and more and more patients are treated on site or online with good results.

A very high percentage of patients who follow the AFOP® method have been cured, others have substantially bettered. There are, though to a much lesser degree, people who have shown to be resistant, be it because of their lack of perseverance or special circumstances.

Currently I am treating children with the AFOP® method (adapted for children and early adolescence) which has had good results, for this reason we have created a special division focused on those below seventeen years of age.

Though this may seem like a form of self-advertisement my deepest intention here is to give back hope to all those people who suffer from this serious disorder, whatever their age, however and whoever they are, wherever they live.

Obsessive disorders can be cured.

23. THE AFOP METHOD FOR THE TREATMENT OF OBSESSIVE DISORDERS:

This method, developed by me, is an acronym of *Activación y Focalización Pulsional,* which in English translates to Drive Activation and Focalization, and has been summed up in this book.

This is about activating primary drives by focalizing them on a passionate objective. In other words, to rekindle life in them and direct it towards concrete objectives which generate sufficient motivation, passions and synergy of energies so as to become the focal point, in the medium and long-term, which guides a person through their life.

So it is not just about activating instincts, the primitive part of the patient, but also, once this has been accomplished, to find a route, a destiny which gives meaning to your own existence.

Your objective is to escape from this mental prison to... to what? To do what? Well... to be who you really are, implicating yourself deeply and daring to live your own life, yours alone.

24. Freeing the monkey and saving the princess?

This is the original title of the book, and though as I wrote this book I changed the title various times, eventually as I finished it I settled back on my original choice. It is the most representative title, and also the most concise, for the work I have done and developed here.

Freeing our inner monkey, our instinctive nature, and integrating (saving) our feminine nature (the princess), thus breaking the hold of a tyrannical, repressive and controlling psyche.

Let us free the animal we have inside, recognize our needs, and be able to heal, accept and integrate the feminine components of the psyche. The *anima* as Carl Gustav Jung would call it.

25. THE SECOND PART:

123

If the readers of this book want to ask me any questions, they can do so by sending them to my personal email address: damianruiz.ps@gmail.com. These will be answered in an upcoming book and would of course remain completely confidential. I think this is the best way to clear up any doubts about the disorder, its course and its possible cure.

in essence this whole book is about life and liberty. Life as the discovery which appears every now and then, life which takes off when you get out of a rut, when you see Paris with youthful eyes, when you travel through Fellini's "La Dolce Vita", when you read a great novel by Vila Matas or Houellebecq for example. When you fall in love and let yourself go, when you reinvent yourself, when you give yourself a night off after having cancelled your previous plans, and sitting in front of the moon and discovering that you love beautiful men or women, or both, or discover music which takes you so far that you will not return to the same places as before. The freedom to think what you feel, and feel what you think, without lying to yourself, without dedicating one more minute apologizing to yourself or others. The freedom to paint your face a thousand and one colours, to dance on the living room floor, to mosh nonsensically during a rock concert, or even during Wagner's Tannhauser, to vibrate taking your spirit in hand and sharing it with the first passer-by who winks at you, to kiss a stranger, to get off the track, to rock up in Buenos Aires, in Rome or New York, ignoring the passing of time and believing in magic.

Because freedom makes it possible to live, love makes it possible to surrender oneself, and freedom makes it possible to write this book.

Thank you.

ACKNOWLEDGEMENTS:

I want to thank my wife Marina for her complete support in the creation of this book, the team at IPITIA for their dedication to this fascinating project, and those people who, over years of professional practise, have placed their trust in me as a psychologist and therapist, to my loyal friends and those members of my family who know the true sense of family.

www.ingramcontent.com/pod-product-compliance
Lightning Source LLC
Chambersburg PA
CBHW070850260726
48661CB00004B/1339